Street Smarts

by Peggy Pancella

Heinemann Library
Chicago, Illinois

Designed by Heinemann Library
Page layout by Roslyn Broder
Printed and bound in the United States of America, North Mankato, MN

12 11 10
9 8 7 6 5 4 3 2

Library of Congress Cataloging-in-Publication Data
Pancella, Peggy.
  Street smarts / Peggy Pancella.
     v. cm. -- (Be safe)
  Includes bibliographical references and index.
  Contents: What is safety? -- Get ready to ride -- Riding safely -- Plan a route -- Walking safely -- Crossing the street -- Street safety -- Dangerous places -- Strangers -- Lost! -- Finding help -- Calling for help -- Be smart and safe -- Safety tips.
  ISBN 1-4034-4933-3 (hardcover) -- ISBN 978-1-4034-4942-9 (pbk.)
  1. Children's accidents--Prevention--Juvenile literature. [1. Safety.] I. Title. II. Series: Pancella, Peggy. Be safe!
  HV675.5.P36 2004
  613.6--dc22
  102010   2003024067
  005957RP

Acknowledgments
The author and publisher are grateful to the following for permission to reproduce copyright material:
Cover photograph by Richard Hutchings/Photo Edit, Inc.
p. 4 Taxi/Getty Images; pp. 5, 16, 17 Tony Freeman/Photo Edit, Inc.; p. 6 Michelle D. Bridwell/Photo Edit, Inc.; pp. 7, 10, 12, 22, 23, 24, 25, 26, 28, 29 David Young-Wolff/Photo Edit, Inc.; pp. 8, 20, 27 Michael Newman/Photo Edit, Inc.; p. 9 Spencer Grant/Photo Edit, Inc.; p. 11 Dennis MacDonald/Photo Edit, Inc.; p. 13 Mary Steinbacher/Photo Edit, Inc.; pp. 14, 18 Davis Barber/Photo Edit, Inc.; p. 15 Bill Aron/Photo Edit, Inc.; p. 19 Jeff Greenberg/Photo Edit, Inc.; p. 21 Barbara Stitzer/Photo Edit, Inc.

Every effort has been made to contact copyright holders of any material reproduced in this book. Any omissions will be rectified in subsequent printings if notice is given to the publisher.

Contents

Some words are shown in bold, **like this.** You can find out what they mean by looking in the glossary.

What Is Safety?

It is important for everyone to stay safe.
Being safe means keeping out of danger.
It means staying away from things or
people that could hurt you.

Safety is important in everything you do. One good time to be safe is when you ride or walk through your neighborhood. Learning some rules to follow can help you stay safe.

Get Ready to Ride

A good way to stay safe in a car is to buckle yourself in. Babies and young children need car seats. Older children and adults should use seat belts instead.

Car seats and belts can help keep you safe in an **accident.** Even a short trip can be dangerous, so always make sure everyone is buckled up before riding.

Riding Safely

When you ride in a car, stay in your car seat or seat belt. Keep your hands and head inside the car. Playing around could cause you to get hurt.

Do not bother the driver, either. He or she needs to pay attention to the road. When the car stops, check for people or cars before opening your door to get out.

Plan a Route

Sometimes you may want to walk places by yourself. Before going out alone, plan a **route** with your parents. They can help you choose the best path to follow.

It is a good idea to practice walking your route with your parents. They can show you where to cross streets and where to go if you have trouble.

Walking Safely

When you leave home, always tell an adult where you are going and when you will return. Walking with a friend can be fun and is safer than walking alone.

Follow your **route** so you do not get lost. Use the sidewalk when you can. If you must walk in the road, stay to the left side, facing traffic. This will help drivers see you more easily.

Crossing the Street

When you cross the street, use a **crosswalk** if there is one. You can also cross at the corner. Stop at the **curb** to look and listen for traffic.

14

Look to the left, then right, then left again. When the road is clear, it is safe to cross. Walk quickly, but do not run! Stay **alert** while you cross.

Street Safety

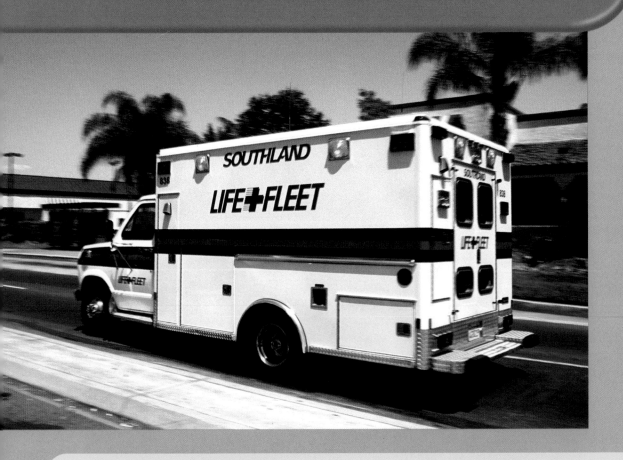

Always be careful near streets. Traffic can be dangerous. Cars and trucks are large and strong. **Emergency vehicles** travel fast. Their **sirens** and lights warn that they are coming.

Even if you do not see any cars, you should not play in the street. Never chase pets or toys into the street, either. Ask an adult for help.

Dangerous Places

Not all places are safe to walk or play. Train tracks and parking lots have **vehicles** that could hurt you. Empty buildings may be falling apart or full of trash.

Some places have "Keep Out" signs, fences, or orange cones to warn you of danger. Always stay away from places like these. Stay in well-lit areas where there are plenty of people.

DANGER
SEWAGE CONTAMINATED
BEACH AND WATER

AVOID SHELLFISH HARVESTING, SWIMMING,
BEACH COMBING, OR OTHER CONTACT ACTIVITIES

Strangers

Sometimes you may see people you do not know in your neighborhood. They are strangers to you. Some strangers are nice, but others could try to hurt you.

If a stranger tries to touch or talk to you, step away and tell a trusted adult. Never go anywhere with strangers. Do not take money or other gifts from them, either.

Lost!

Even the most careful people sometimes get lost. You may feel scared or upset if this happens to you. Try to stay calm and think clearly.

If someone was with you, stay where you are. The person might come back to find you. If you were alone, or if you feel unsafe, look for help right away.

Finding Help

If you feel lost or unsafe, go for help. Find a safe place with lots of people around, such as a store or **restaurant**. Look for an adult who can help.

Try to find an adult that you feel you can trust. Police officers are very helpful people. Women with children and store workers are usually safe to ask, too.

Calling for Help

Pay phones can be helpful, too. Always carry enough money for a phone call. If you know the number of a parent or trusted adult, put your money in, and dial.

If you do not have money, you can call **911** for free. Say you need help and answer the **operator's** questions. Operators can figure out where you are and send help.

Be Smart and Safe

You should be prepared whenever you walk. Wear clothing that is right for the day's weather. After dark, wear light-colored clothes and stay in well-lit areas.

Pay attention to things around you. Tell an adult if anything seems unusual or strange. Most of all, walk tall and proud. Being safe can also be fun!

Safety Tips

- Always ride safely—buckle up!

- Plan and practice a safe **route** for walking alone.

- Listen for traffic and look both ways before crossing a street. Use a **crosswalk** if you can.

- Stay away from people or places that might be dangerous. If you have a problem or something does not feel right, tell an adult you trust.

- **Memorize** important phone numbers and carry enough money to make a phone call.

Glossary

911 phone number to dial in an emergency

accident something that happens unexpectedly

alert paying attention to things around you

crosswalk place on a street where you can safely cross to the other side

curb raised edge along the side of the street

emergency sudden event that forces you to act quickly

memorize learn by heart

operator person whose job is to give help or information over the telephone

pay phone public telephone that takes money

restaurant public eating place

route path you take to get somewhere

siren kind of loud warning signal

vehicle something that carries people or supplies from one place to another

Index